Little Pig Figwort

To the memory of Henrietta B and
to all sleepless piglets around the world.

C. M.

First published in paperback in Great Britain by Collins Picture Books in 2001
1 3 5 7 9 10 8 6 4 2
ISBN: 978 0 00 664699 0
Collins is an imprint of HarperCollins Children's Books, Part of HarperCollins*Publishers* Ltd.
Text copyright © Henrietta Branford 2000
Illustrations copyright © Claudio Muñoz 2000
The author and illustrator assert the moral right to be identified as the author and illustrator of the work.
A CIP catalogue record for this title is available from the British Library.

The HarperCollins website address is: www.harpercollins.co.uk

Printed in China.

Little Pig Figwort

Henrietta Branford
illustrated by Claudio Muñoz

HarperCollins *Children's Books*

Deep in a heap the little pigs sleep – Dill,
Chive and Caraway, Tansy and Pansy,
and smallest of allest, Pig Figwort.

"Sleep tight, little pigs," says Pig Mama.

"All night, little pigs," says Pig Papa.

Dill, Chive and Caraway, Tansy and Pansy
snuggled and snoozed, cosy and comfy and soon
deep asleep, sweet-dreaming the night away.

But little Pig Figwort could not get to sleep.

He opened one eye.

He opened the other eye.

He tossed and he turned,
he wriggled and he jiggled,

he tried and he tried,

but he could not get to sleep.

"I am a pig who likes to have fun," said little Pig Figwort.

"What I need is an adventure. What I need
is a deep-sea dive in my submarine."
Little Pig Figwort hopped out of bed.

He pulled on his deep-sea diving suit
and squeezed into his submarine.

"Down periscope, dive, dive, dive!" he shouted and...

…he shot right down to the bottom of the sea, past an octopus sucking his thumbs, and a snoozing whale, past a sunken wreck, down to the bottom where the mermaids race and the starfish shimmer.

"Ready, steady, go! Now for some fun!" shouted little Pig Figwort.

But the mermaids weren't racing, and the starfish weren't playing either.

"Shush, Pig Figwort," whispered a sleepy little mermaid. "Don't you know it's night time?"

She flicked her tail at him and tucked her seaweed blanket under her chin.

"Shush, little Pig Figwort," whispered
a starfish. "It's night time, go home!"
  "Bother," said little Pig Figwort.
He squeezed into his submarine
and headed for home.

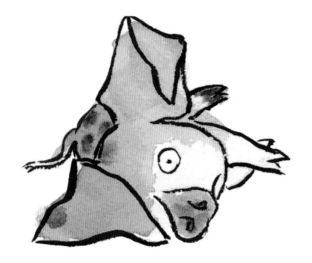

He snuggled down.
He shut one eye.

He shut the other eye.

He tossed and he turned,
he wriggled and he jiggled,

he tried and he tried,

but he could not get to sleep.

"The trouble is, I'm still not
sleepy," said little Pig Figwort.
"What I need is more adventure."

"What I need is a trip to the North Pole."
He zipped up his snow suit and started
up his skidoo.

"Ice and snow! Here I go!" shouted little Pig
Figwort, and he drove his skidoo faster than fast…
up and over snow mountains and across glittering
glaciers to the far North Pole where the polar bears
sledge and the seals play hide and seek.

But the seals weren't hiding. They had all gone home to bed. And the polar bears weren't sledging. They were snoozing all in a heap.

DO NOT DISTURB

"Go 'way Pig Figwort!" growled a big old bear. "Can't you see we're sleeping?"

"Bother," said little Pig Figwort.
He hopped back on his skidoo
and drove all the way home.

He snuggled down.
He shut one eye.

He shut the other eye.

He tossed and he turned,
he wriggled and he jiggled,

he tried and he tried,
but he could not get to sleep.

"The trouble is, I'm just not sleepy
at all," sighed little Pig Figwort.

"What I need is something really
truly exciting. What I need is a trip to…

...the **moon**."

He snapped on his space suit
and climbed into his rocket.
"Five, four,
three, two
one, **blast off!**"
shouted little Pig Figwort.

He shot over the treetops, higher than houses, higher than aeroplanes, up to the moon where pigs fly high in the silver sky all night, because it's much too shiny bright to sleep.

Little Pig Figwort flew with the moon pigs.

He looped the loop with them,

he ran races,

he played snoutball

and tag, and hide and seek.

He played Pig Pirates,

Moon Jump,

and
Rocket
Races.

He played and he played and when he just couldn't play any more, he tumbled back into his rocket and flew home.

"That was fun," said little Pig Figwort, back in bed.

"That was so much fun that I don't think I'll ever go to sleep again."

Little Pig Figwort shut one eye.

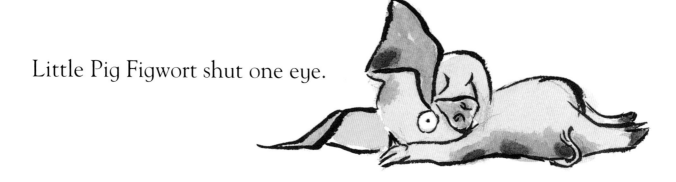

He shut the other eye.

He cuddled

and muddled

down into the heap...

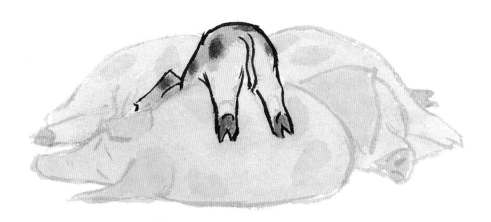

Shhhh...

little Pig Figwort is fast asleep.